D1302827

infographics
HOW IT WORKS

YOUR BODY

JON RICHARDS AND ED SIMKINS

 Gareth Stevens
PUBLISHING

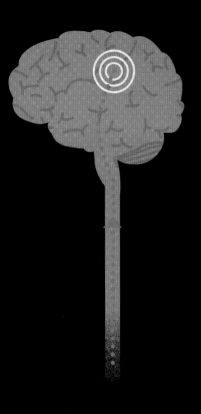

Please visit our website,
www.garethstevens.com.
For a free color catalog of all our
high-quality books, call toll free
1-800-542-2595 or fax 1-877-542-2596.

CATALOGING-IN-PUBLICATION DATA

Names: Richards, Jon. | Simkins, Ed.
 Title: Your body / Jon Richards and
 Ed Simkins.
Description: New York : Gareth Stevens
 Publishing, 2018. | Series: Infographics:
 how it works | Includes index.
Identifiers: ISBN 9781538214398 (pbk.) |
 ISBN 9781538213667 (library bound) |
 ISBN 9781538214404 (6 pack)
 Subjects: LCSH: Human body--Juvenile
 literature. | Human biology--Juvenile
 literature.
Classification: LCC QP37.R47 2018 |
 DDC 612--dc23

Published in 2018 by
Gareth Stevens Publishing
11 East 14th Street, Suite 349
New York, NY 10003

Copyright © 2018 Wayland, a division
of Hachette Children's Group

Editor: Liza Miller
Produced by Tall Tree Ltd
Editor: Jon Richards
Designer: Ed Simkins

Printed in China
CPSIA compliance information: Batch CW18GS:
For further information contact Gareth Stevens,
New York, New York at 1-800-542-2595.

CONTENTS

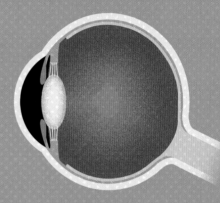

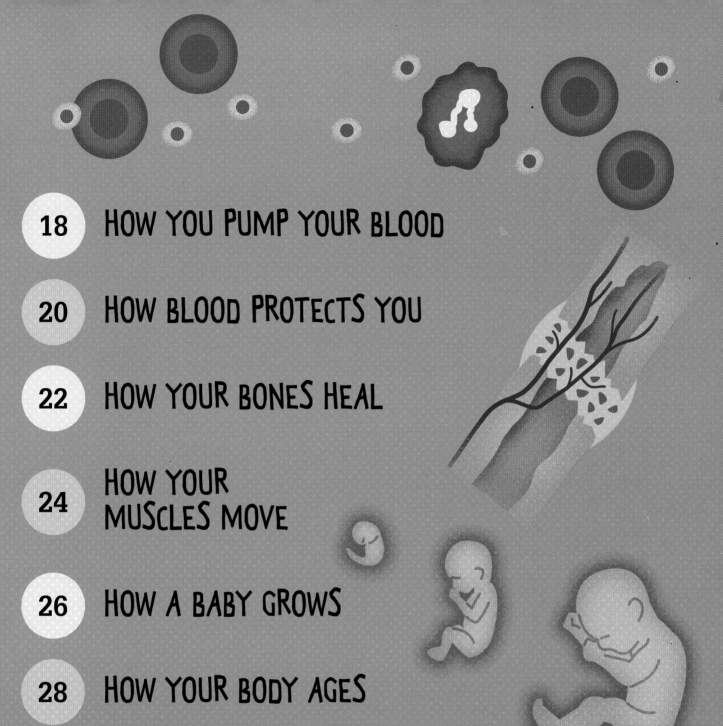

YOUR AMAZING BODY

The human body is a very complicated network of systems and processes that are all designed to keep you alive. These systems take what you need out of the air around you and the food you eat, and get rid of anything your body doesn't want or need.

CELLS TO SYSTEMS

The smallest unit that forms part of your body is a cell. Similar cells are arranged together to create tissues, which carry out a specific job. For example, muscle tissue is designed to contract, or get shorter. Tissues are collected together to form organs, such as the heart or lungs, while organs are grouped together to form systems, such as the digestive system.

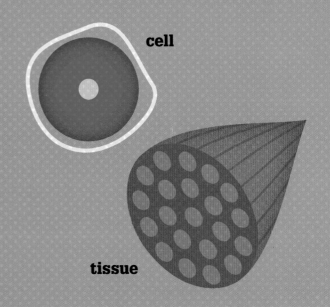

cell

tissue

CHEMICALS

Your body is a chemical soup, made up of dozens of different elements. Most of it is made up of oxygen, but an adult contains enough carbon to fill about 900 pencils and enough phosphorus to make 220 matches.

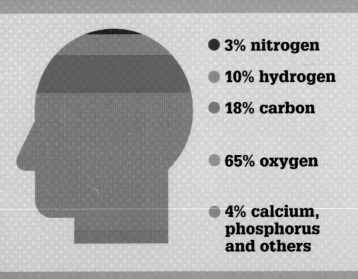

- 3% nitrogen
- 10% hydrogen
- 18% carbon
- 65% oxygen
- 4% calcium, phosphorus and others

You lose about 8 pounds (4 kg) of skin cells every year.

Your heart will beat about three billion times during your lifetime.

There are about 100 trillion cells in a human body. However, there are ten times this number of tiny bacteria living in your guts, helping to break down your food.

organ

system

HOW YOUR EYES SEE

During the day, your eyes are able to detect the size, shape, and color of objects around you. At night, with no sun to light everything, objects appear dark and gray.

① LIGHT RAYS

Rays of light pass into the eye through a clear front layer called the cornea. This bends the light rays so that they can be brought into focus by the lens.

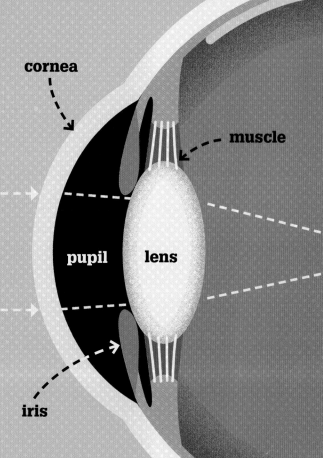

cornea

muscle

light rays

pupil

lens

iris

② PUPIL

The light rays enter the eye through a hole in the front called the pupil. The iris adjusts to make the pupil smaller to let less light into the eye if things are bright, or larger to let more light into the eye if things are dark.

③ LENS

Behind the pupil is the lens. Muscles pull the lens, making it thinner or thicker, so that it can focus the light rays and produce a sharp picture.

Stand in a dimly lit room and look closely at a friend's eyes to see how big their pupils are. Now turn the lights on and see what happens to the size of their pupils!

❹ EYEBALL

The light rays pass through the eyeball, which is filled with a gel called the vitreous humor.

❺ IMAGE

The light rays cross over and hit the back of the eye, called the retina. This is covered with millions of light-sensitive cells called photoreceptors. These convert the upside-down image into nerve signals.

vitreous humor

image

optic nerve

There are two types of photoreceptors. Cone cells detect different colors and are used in bright conditions. Rod cells are used when it is dark. They cannot detect colors, which is why you see inky grays at nighttime.

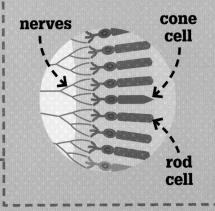

nerves

cone cell

rod cell

❻ SIGNAL

These nerve signals are sent along the optic nerve to an area at the back of the brain called the visual cortex. Here, the signals are interpreted and the image is "seen" the right way up.

visual cortex

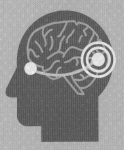

HOW YOUR EARS HEAR

Sounds travel through the air as waves. Your ears contain organs which can detect these waves and turn them into signals to send to your brain.

❶ SOUND

Sound waves pass down the ear canal.

ear canal

sound waves

eardrum

ear bones

❷ EARDRUM

The eardrum starts to vibrate as the sound waves hit it.

❸ TINY BONES

The other side of the eardrum is attached to three tiny bones, which pass these vibrations on to a spiral-shaped tube called the cochlea.

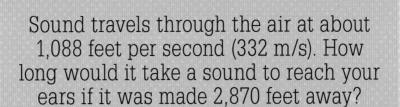
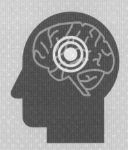

auditory cortex

Sound travels through the air at about 1,088 feet per second (332 m/s). How long would it take a sound to reach your ears if it was made 2,870 feet away?

auditory nerves

6 SIGNALS

The nerve signals pass along the auditory nerves to a part of the brain called the auditory cortex, where the signals are interpreted and the sounds are "heard."

5 TINY HAIRS

The cochlea also has thousands of tiny hairs, which wave back and forth as the fluid moves. These hairs trigger nerve signals.

cochlea

4 COCHLEA

The inside of the cochlea is filled with fluid. The vibrations make this fluid move.

hairs

This is the eustachian tube. It connects the ear to the back of the nose.

fluid

9

HOW YOU SMELL AND TASTE

Your nose and tongue detect chemicals in the air and in your food, allowing you to smell odors and taste what you are eating.

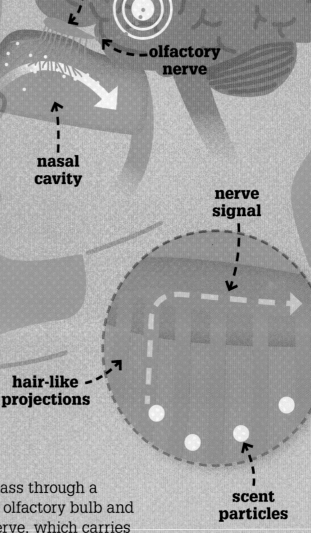

olfactory bulb

brain

olfactory nerve

nasal cavity

scent particles

nerve signal

hair-like projections

scent particles

❶ BREATHE IN

When you breathe in through your nose, air carrying scent particles flows into your nasal passages and up into a space inside your skull called the nasal cavity.

❷ SCENT

In the roof of the nasal cavity are millions of tiny hair-like projections. These trap the scent particles, triggering nerve signals.

❸ BULB

The nerve signals pass through a structure called the olfactory bulb and into the olfactory nerve, which carries them to parts of the brain where the odor is "smelled."

❶ TONGUE

Different flavors are detected by tiny sensors called taste buds, which are found on your tongue and in other parts of your mouth.

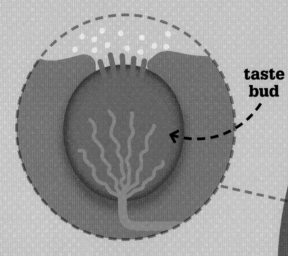

taste bud

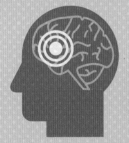

❷ TASTE BUDS

The taste buds send signals to a part of the brain called the gustatory cortex, where the flavors are "tasted."

gustatory cortex

There are five different types of flavors.

sweet **sour** **bitter** **salty** **umami**

TRY THIS...

Your sense of smell is closely linked to how you taste. Ask a friend to close their eyes, hold their nose, and then taste various foods. See how many they guess correctly!

11

HOW YOU FEEL

Just beneath the surface of your skin are millions of tiny sensors. These detect changes in touch and temperature, and send signals to the brain about everything you come into contact with.

❶ FINGERTIP

Your finger touches something sharp. This triggers sensors in the fingertips, which send signals to the brain along sensory nerves.

❹ PAIN

The sense signal travels to a part of the brain known as the sensory cortex, where the signal is interpreted and the pain is "felt."

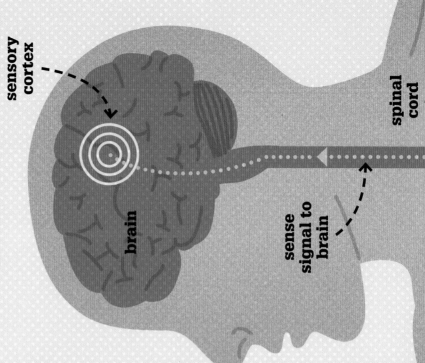

sensory cortex

brain

spinal cord

sense signal to brain

motor nerve

3 THE BRAIN

At the same time, the sense signal continues on towards the brain.

sense signal to brain

spinal cord

motor nerve

muscle

sensory nerves

2 SPINE

When the signal enters the spinal cord, another signal is sent along a motor nerve back to the arm. This causes a reflex reaction so you pull your finger away from the source of pain.

TRY THIS...

Test your reflexes. Cross one leg over the knee of the other. Now ask a friend to tap just below the kneecap of your top leg and watch as it twitches with a reflex reaction.

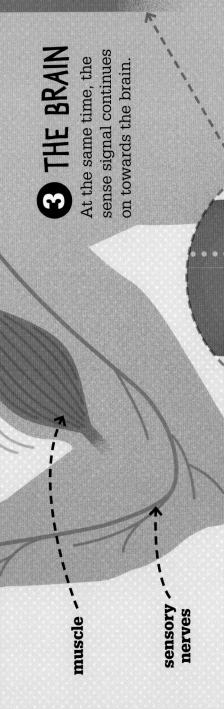

The longest nerve in your body runs from the tip of your toe, all the way up your leg and into the base of your spinal cord.

sciatic nerve

HOW YOUR BODY DIGESTS FOOD

Running through your body is a long, twisting tube that is divided into different sections. This tube takes the food you eat and processes it so your body can take out any nutrients. It then helps to get rid of any unwanted material.

piece of food

❶ DOWN THE HATCH

Inside your mouth, your teeth and tongue chop food up, grind it, and mix it with saliva to create a paste. This is then swallowed down your food pipe, or esophagus, into your stomach.

esophagus

stomach

❷ CHURN

Muscles in your stomach churn the food up and mix it with chemicals released by the stomach wall. These chemicals start to break the food down. The mixture then moves into the small intestine.

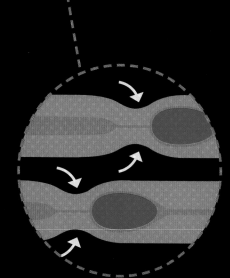

Muscles push food along the esophagus.

❸ ENZYMES

Chemicals called enzymes get to work breaking up parts of the food into smaller and smaller pieces until they are simple enough for your body to absorb.

food particle

enzyme

The enzyme attaches to the food particle.

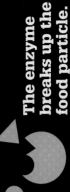

The enzyme breaks up the food particle.

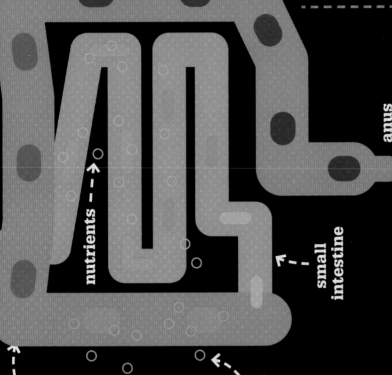

large intestine

nutrients -- →

small intestine

water

anus

❹ ABSORBED

By the time any remaining food enters the large intestine, most of the nutrients have been taken into the body. The large intestine absorbs water, leaving behind a mixture of unwanted material.

❺ POOP

This unwanted material leaves your body as poop, or feces, through your anus.

TRY THIS . . .

Put some food into your mouth and chew it for 30 seconds. Now spit it out into a bowl and see how your teeth, tongue, and saliva have mashed the food into a paste.

HOW YOU BREATHE

Inside your chest are two sacs called lungs. These draw air into your body and absorb oxygen, which your body needs to live. The lungs also get rid of carbon dioxide, which is a waste product of your body's energy-making process.

① MUSCLES

Muscles in between your ribs contract to pull the ribcage up, while a sheet of muscle below the lungs called the diaphragm also contracts. This makes the lungs bigger and draws air into them.

muscles

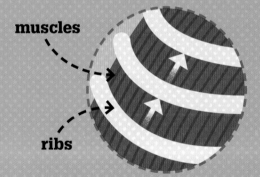

ribs

② AIR IN

Air enters the body through either the nose or the mouth, and passes into the windpipe, or trachea, that runs down the front of your neck.

trachea

lung

③ LUNGS

As the air enters the chest, the trachea splits in two, with one pipe going into each lung.

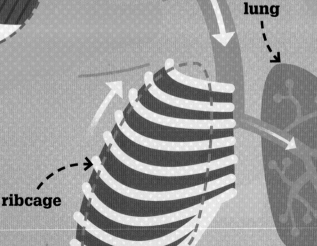

ribcage

diaphragm

Try to blow up a balloon as much as you can with a single breath. Compare your balloon with balloons blown up by your friends. The person who blew up their balloon the most probably has the largest lung capacity.

④ TINY SACS

As the air travels further into the lungs, the pipes divide again and again, getting thinner and thinner, until they end at tiny sacs, which are called alveoli.

The alveoli increase the surface area inside your lungs. In fact, your lungs have an internal surface area the size of half a tennis court!

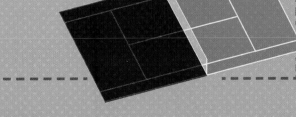

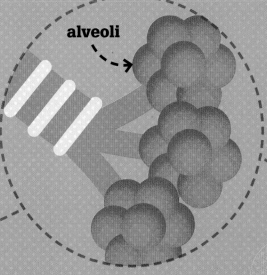

alveoli

⑤ BLOOD

Inside the alveoli, oxygen passes from the air into the blood, while carbon dioxide passes the other way.

⑥ BREATHE OUT

The muscles between the ribs and in the diaphragm then relax, pushing on the lungs and squeezing the air out of them as you breathe out.

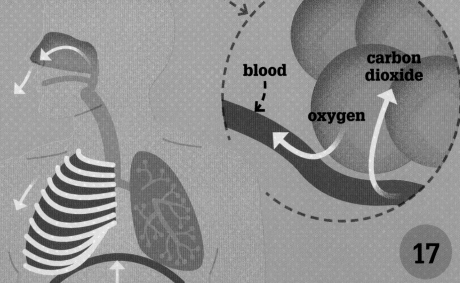

blood

carbon dioxide

oxygen

HOW YOU PUMP YOUR BLOOD

Sitting in between your two lungs is your heart. This muscular sac beats all the time, pushing blood around your body. Oxygen is collected from your lungs and carried, along with important nutrients, to every one of your cells.

Your heart will beat about 60–90 times a minute while you are resting. This rate will increase when you exercise to push more blood and nutrients to your muscles.

2 IN THE LUNGS

Inside the lungs, the blood collects oxygen and gets rid of carbon dioxide. Blood then goes back to the heart through the pulmonary veins.

lung

1 TO THE LUNGS

Blood is pushed out of your heart into the pulmonary arteries and towards the lungs.

pulmonary arteries

6 IN THE VEINS

The blood travels back to your heart along veins, such as the vena cava. Inside the heart, it is pushed out into the pulmonary arteries to begin the cycle again.

vena cava

veins

5 GIVING OXYGEN

As the blood flows through the capillaries, it delivers oxygen and nutrients to your body's cells and collects waste products, such as carbon dioxide.

lung

aorta

pulmonary
veins

heart

arteries

capillaries

TRY THIS...

Find your pulse on your wrist — this is caused by your heart pushing blood through your blood vessels. Count how many times it beats in a minute, then run around for one minute. How does this exercise affect your pulse rate?

❸ BLOOD OUT

After entering the heart, blood is pushed out again into the body's largest artery, called the aorta. This splits up into smaller arteries, which branch out to all parts of the body.

Arteries have thick walls to carry high-pressure blood away from the heart. Veins have thin walls to carry low-pressure blood back to the heart. Capillaries have very thin walls so that oxygen and nutrients can pass through them.

artery

vein

capillary

❹ GETTING SMALLER

As the blood is pushed along, it flows into smaller and smaller blood vessels, before it enters tiny capillaries.

HOW BLOOD PROTECTS YOU

As well as carrying oxygen and nutrients around your body, blood plays an important role in protecting you. It blocks up wounds to stop blood loss and start the healing process, and it fights off invaders that can make you sick.

Blood contains three types of cells: red cells, white cells, and platelets. Red blood cells carry oxygen and nutrients. White blood cells help to fight invaders and prevent infections. Platelets are tiny cell fragments that play an important role in blood clotting.

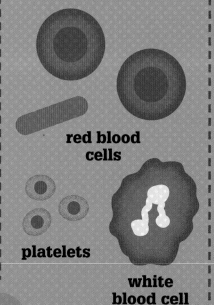

red blood cells

platelets

white blood cell

❶ OUCH!

When blood is exposed by a wound, the tiny platelets start to change, creating sticky fibers that join together to form a net.

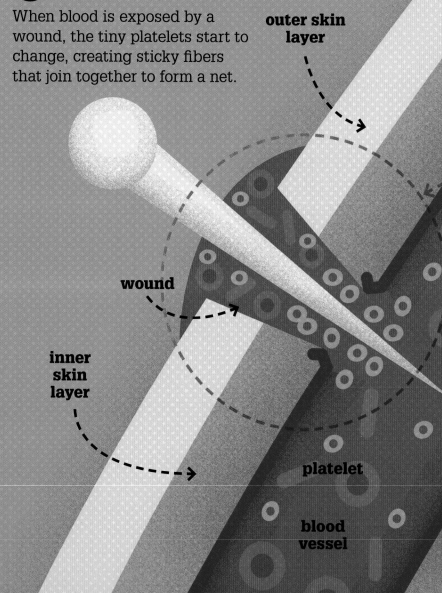

outer skin layer

wound

inner skin layer

platelet

blood vessel

Your body produces 2.5 million red blood cells every second. How many are produced in a minute?

clot

❷ CLOT

This sticky net traps red blood cells, creating a clot which blocks and covers the wound.

scab

❸ SCAB

The clot dries and forms a hard scab, which covers and protects the wound.

wound closed

❹ HEALING

Beneath the protective scab, skin cells regrow to close and heal the wound.

HOW YOUR BONES HEAL

The bones that make up your skeleton are incredibly strong, but can be quite flexible to withstand everyday knocks and bumps. However, if a force is too great, they can fracture or break.

1 BREAK

As soon as a break occurs, your bones start the healing process. A blood clot forms around the break as well as a swelling, or callus. This protects the injury while it heals.

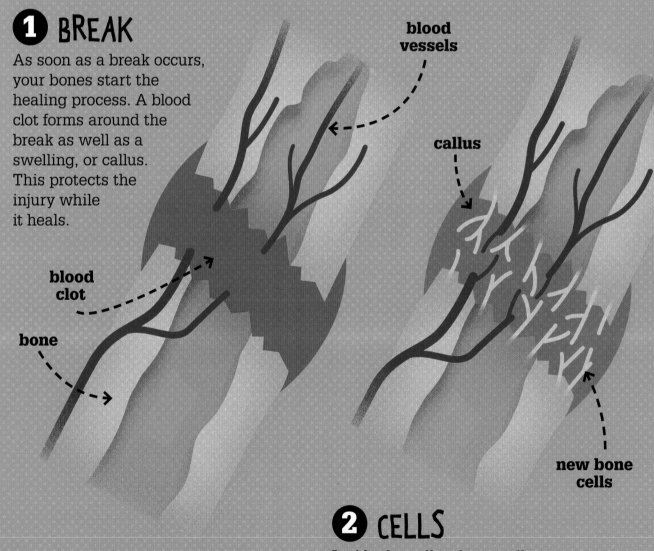

blood vessels

callus

blood clot

bone

new bone cells

2 CELLS

Inside the callus, bone cells start to grow across the break from both sides.

In many fractures, doctors set the broken bone in a plaster cast or a special plastic case. If the fracture is really bad, they may even put metal pins in the bones. Why do you think this is?

A cube of bone tissue, measuring about 1 inch (2.5 cm) on each side, could bear a load of more than 10 tons (9.5 metric tons)! That makes it four times stronger than concrete.

❸ HEALS

Bone tissue continues to grow across the break until the fracture heals.

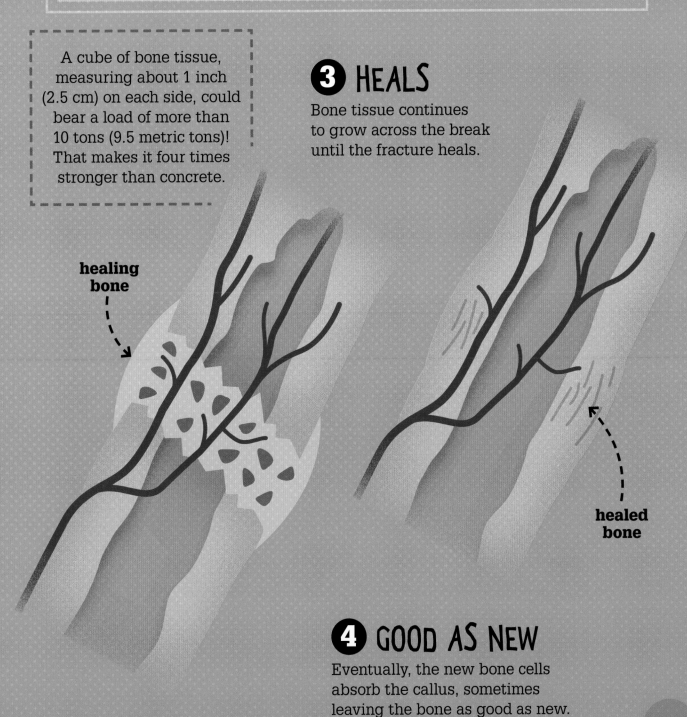

healing bone

healed bone

❹ GOOD AS NEW

Eventually, the new bone cells absorb the callus, sometimes leaving the bone as good as new.

23

HOW YOUR
MUSCLES MOVE

Beneath your skin are hundreds of muscles.
These body parts can get shorter,
or contract, to pull on your bones
so you move around.

1 TINY FIBERS

The muscles that are attached
to your bones are made up of
millions of tiny fibers that
lie in bands next to
each other.

nerve

bicep
contracts

fibers

forearm
bones

tricep
relaxes

elbow

There are three types of muscles in your body: skeletal, smooth, and cardiac. Skeletal muscles are attached to bones. Smooth muscles are found in various body parts, including your guts, where they push food along. Cardiac muscles keep your heart beating.

❹ WORKING IN PAIRS

Because muscles can only pull, they are usually arranged in teams of two or more so that they can move body parts in more than one direction. To straighten the arm, the tricep muscle contracts, and the bicep muscle relaxes.

bicep relaxes

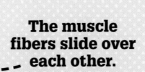

tricep contracts

❷ SIGNAL

When a muscle receives a nerve signal to contract, these fibers slide over each other, making the muscle shorter.

The muscle fibers slide over each other.

❸ PULL

As the muscle shortens, it pulls on a bone, making that bone move. In this case, the biceps muscle is pulling on the forearm bones, making the arm bend at the elbow.

TRY THIS...

Put your hand around the upper arm of a friend and feel how the muscles above and below the arm contract to bend and straighten it.

HOW A BABY GROWS

After sex cells have fused together in a process called fertilization, an amazing series of changes begins. A single cell eventually develops into a baby in the mother's womb.

❶ DIVIDES

About 30 hours after fertilization, the single cell divides into two different cells. It keeps dividing, doubling the number of cells each time. Around 12 days after fertilization, there are about 1,000 cells grouped in a clump.

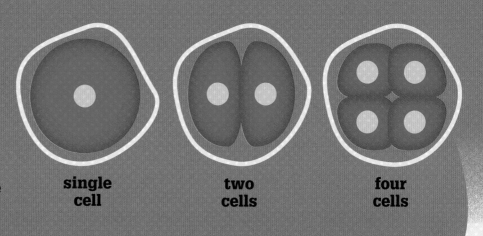

single cell

two cells

four cells

❷ ARM BUDS

About 4 weeks after fertilization, a head and backbone have developed, as well as tiny buds, which will eventually become the arms and legs.

❸ EYES

By 14 weeks after fertilization, the fetus is nearly 4 inches (10 cm) long. It can move its eyes, although the eyelids stay closed at this stage. All the internal organs are in the right place and the bones start to harden.

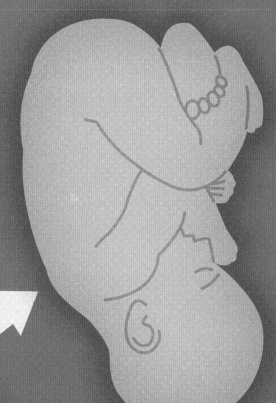

6 READY

About 38 weeks after fertilization, the baby is ready to be born. Chemicals called hormones are released, which prompt the mother's womb to start contracting.

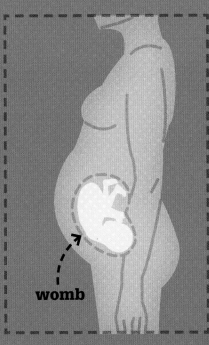

womb

5 TURNING

About 30 weeks after fertilization, the eyes may open. By 34 weeks, most babies have moved around so that their heads are pointing down, ready for birth.

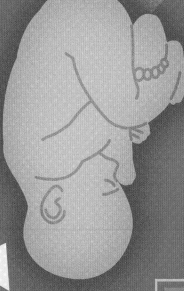

4 LUNGS

By about 26 weeks after fertilization, the lungs are ready to breathe air (although the fetus won't breathe air until it is born) and eyelashes and fingernails have developed.

TRY THIS...

If cells divide and their numbers double every hour, calculate how many cells there would be 8 hours after the first cell has formed.

HOW YOUR BODY AGES

As you get older, your body goes through some amazing changes. You will grow bigger throughout childhood until maturity, and then your body will start to weaken as you age.

At birth, a baby will have 350 bones in their skeleton. As the child grows, some of these bones will fuse together. By the time they are an adult, they will have 206 bones.

❶ BABY

A baby's body grows quickly. As a young child, you will learn basic skills, such as walking and talking.

❷ CHILD

During childhood, your body will grow in size, increasing in height and weight. You will also lose your baby teeth and gain adult teeth.

❸ TEENAGER

During adolescence, your body will go through puberty as it gets ready for adult life and the possibility of having children.

When a child is born, its head makes up one-quarter of its body length. By the time they are an adult, it will only make up one-eighth of their body length.

4 ADULT

After puberty, your body has reached maturity and stopped growing. You may start a family of your own.

5 OLD AGE

As you get old, your body will become weaker and some body parts will not work as well as they did when you were younger.

TRY THIS...

Measure the heights of everyone in your class and write them down in order from tallest to shortest. Can you work out the average height for your class?

GLOSSARY

ANUS

The opening at the end of the large intestine through which solid waste matter leaves the body.

BACTERIA

A group of microorganisms. Some can cause disease, but others perform important roles in the gut, helping to digest food.

CARDIAC

Relating to the heart.

CELL

The smallest building block of life. All animals and plants are made out of cells. The human body contains about 100 trillion cells.

DIAPHRAGM

A sheet of muscle that sits across the bottom of the ribs and helps you to breathe.

ENZYMES

Special chemicals that speed up certain reactions.

FERTILIZATION

When male and female sex cells fuse together to make new babies.

FETUS

The name given to a developing baby from the ninth week after fertilization until its birth.

GUSTATORY

Relating to taste. The gustatory system refers to the mouth cavity, the tongue and its sense of taste.

HORMONES

Special chemicals released by organs telling parts of your body how to behave.

MOLECULES

A group of atoms that are bonded (joined) together. These include the carbon, hydrogen, and oxygen atoms that form a glucose molecule.

MOTOR NERVE

A type of long cell that runs through the spine and carries messages to the body's muscles in the form of tiny electrical signals.

MUSCLE

A type of soft tissue that contracts, or gets shorter, to produce force or movement.

NASAL

Relating to the nose. The nasal cavity is the large air-filled space behind the nose.

NERVE SIGNALS

Small electrical signals that travel along nerve cells, carrying information to the brain from sensors all over the body. They also carry instructions from the brain to different organs and muscles, telling them what to do.

NUTRIENTS

Substances such as carbohydrates, proteins, or fats that are obtained from food and are essential for normal body functioning.

ODOR

A distinctive smell, especially an unpleasant one. Odors are made up of chemical compounds.

OLFACTORY

Describes something relating to smell. Olfaction is the sense of smell. Humans detect smell when odorant molecules come into contact with olfactory sensors located in the nasal cavity.

OXYGEN

A gas found in air that is breathed in, absorbed by the bloodstream, and used by cells to release energy from glucose.

PUBERTY

A period of body development that starts at around age 12 in girls and 14 in boys. During puberty, the body grows very quickly, changes shape, and develops sex organs.

PULMONARY

Relating to the lungs. A pulmonary artery carries blood from the heart to the lungs.

PULSE

The regular beating in your blood vessels caused by blood being pumped around your body by your heart.

REFLEX

A reaction that can be performed without thought, such as changing the size of your pupil when the light levels change.

SALIVA

A watery liquid secreted into the mouth by glands. Saliva makes food slippery for chewing and swallowing, and helps to digest food.

SENSORY NERVE

A type of long cell that carries messages from the body's sense organs towards the spine and brain in the form of tiny electrical signals.

SPINAL CORD

The long thin tube of nerve tissue that extends from the brain and down the middle of the back. The spinal cord controls many of the body's automatic actions and reflexes.

UMAMI

One of the five basic tastes, umami is said to have a pleasant savory flavor and is found in mushrooms, cheese, meats and soy sauce.

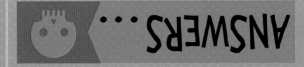

ANSWERS...

8-9 It would take a sound 2.6 seconds to travel 2,870 feet.

18-19 You will find that your pulse gets quicker after you exercise.

20-21 Your body produces about 150 million red blood cells every minute!

22-23 The cast, case, or pins will help to keep the broken bone in the correct position while it heals.

26-27 There will be 256 cells after eight hours.

31

INDEX

WEBSITES

kids.nationalgeographic.com/games/quizzes/quiz-whiz-human-body/

Test your knowledge of the human body with this fun quiz!

www.dkfindout.com/us/human-body/your-amazing-body/

Learn even more about your amazing body here!